Children of the GREAT HUNGER

Bradán

Text by David Ross
Illustrated by Robert Farley

© 2002 Waverley Books Ltd

Published for Waverley Books Ltd by Geddes & Grosset,
David Dale House, New Lanark, ML11 9DJ, Scotland

ISBN 1 902407 23 7

Printed and bound in China

Children of the
GREAT HUNGER

CHAPTER ONE: A LUCKY GIRL

I DID not know I was lucky until the Matron of the workhouse told me: "You're a very lucky girl, Mary O'Donnell."

I had been brought to her office, where there was another lady, in a big coat and hat.

"This is Mrs Palmer. She is looking for a servant and I have decided that you may be suitable. Mrs Palmer will try you for a week. Work hard, Mary. If you don't suit Mrs Palmer, she won't keep you. And you won't be able to come back here."

Mrs Palmer looked at me.

"Is she healthy?" she asked.

"Indeed, ma'am. Mary had the fever, but she recovered from it."

"And is she strong?" she asked.

"Strong enough, ma'am. A little more feeding than we can manage here will soon put more flesh on her bones."

The lady frowned.

"I don't like to spoil the servants," she said. "Is she biddable?"

"Oh, you may be sure of it, ma'am."

The Matron's voice went low.

"She's very young. You can train her into obedience. She came here with the mother and a brother and sister, but they took the fever and died. She has no one."

She turned to me.

"You can go now, Mary. Mrs Palmer will come to fetch you tomorrow. Give her a curtsy, now."

Back in the girls' yard I told my friends what had happened. They thought I was lucky, too.

"Oh, Mary! What will you get to eat?"

"Maybe she'll get new bread. And meat, even!"

"Does the lady have a grand house?"

"Will you remember us, Mary, when you're having great feeds of bread and beef?"

I looked at my friends' white, thin faces.

"I'll never forget you," I said.

IT IS strange to think that once I was happy. We lived on a beautiful, green, Irish hillside, and we could look down our valley to the sea, and up our valley to the blue mountains. We had our little house, and goats, and a pig we called "Big Turk". In a row stretching along the slope were ten or eleven other houses, just like our own, with families the same as ourselves. On the hill around the houses were plots of land, planted with potatoes and oats. Each little house had a turf stack

beside it, brought down from the bog, to keep its fire going. Down at the lower end of the valley, near the sea, was a big white house with trees all round. That was where the Proprietor lived. For a long time I thought a Proprietor was a sort of giant. I used to think if we strayed too far from the house he would catch us and eat us. That was before I got older and knew that the Proprietor was the man who owned all the land round about.

My mammy and daddy worked hard on the land. They would walk down to the sea-shore with creels on their backs, and walk back up the hill laden with seaweed, or shelly sand, to spread on the earth and make it fertile. I was the eldest, and it was my job to mind the goats, and my sister and brother, Bridget and Brian. When it was time to dig up the potatoes, we all helped. My daddy had a big, long-handled spade and he pushed it carefully into the ground.

"We don't want to split the praties," he would say. "We want to keep them round and whole, so that they'll last."

We loved to kneel down by him, watching the potatoes appear as the earth was turned up, and grabbing for them to put them in the creel.

"Careful, now. Careful," my daddy said. "We

want them all. Not just the big ones." We children always missed a few, but my mammy came along after us, sifting through the soft earth again, making sure that every single one was picked out.

"Bless the potato," my daddy said. "It is our bread and our beef. No one in Ireland need ever go hungry when he can grow potatoes."

For potatoes was what we lived on, every day. The oats were mostly grown to sell, so that we could pay the Proprietor his rent. Sometimes we had fish, or mussels, and maybe two or three times in the year we had meat. For Christmas and Shrove Tuesday, we always had a bit of mutton or a hen.

That night, with the first of the potatoes, we'd have a feast, and then others would come along to our house, and there would be singing, and stories, and one man had a fiddle on which he played lovely tunes, that went on until we children were so tired we could no longer stay awake.

CHAPTER THREE: THE BLIGHT

THE first time I heard the words "potato blight", I didn't know what they meant. I had never heard the word "blight" before. My mammy and daddy were talking about it.

"There have been bad years before," my mammy said.

"It's over half the country, and more," said my daddy. "The crops are rotting in the fields."

My mammy looked out to where our potatoes were growing, the strong green stalks and the creamy-white flowers.

"Well, our own are looking fine," she said.

All through that summer we watched our potatoes. We heard frightening stories about other places, where the people would have no food for the winter, because the terrible disease of potato blight had ruined their crop. Our own looked fine, right through until it was at last time to lift them. We had been through the hungry summer months, when the old potatoes are nearly all gone, and the new ones not ready, and there isn't much to eat, except oatmeal, and we were looking forward to our first feast of the new potatoes.

Happily we grubbed up the shiny new potatoes from the soil. But then I heard our mammy cry out. Our daddy dropped his spade and came running up.

Even as they appeared in the daylight, the potatoes were turning black.

"Quick," cried Daddy. "Sort out the good ones. Maybe it's just a few."

Hastily we scrabbled through the creel, trying to find potatoes that did not have the spreading black marks. But even the ones that we took out soon began to turn black. In a few hours time, the whole crop had turned soft and rotten. They smelled horrible. Our neighbours came around, and their faces told us the same thing had happened to them. The faces of the men and women were grim and serious. We children stood apart, but we heard them talking, and the heard the name of the Proprietor mentioned many times. Then my daddy and two other men set off down the valley towards the big white house.

"What are they doing, Mammy?" I asked.

"They have gone to see the Proprietor, and tell him about the potato blight, that it is here too. We have paid him a good rent all these years, now it will be his turn to help us. We must have food."

It was a sad and small meal that night, with no music or stories. The Proprietor had said there was nothing he could do. He said it was a problem for the whole nation.

Our daddy was very angry.

"I will not see my children starve!" he cried out.

"Hush," said our mammy. "It will never come to that. Something will have to be done."

WE DID not starve in that first winter. But we went to bed every night hungry. We used to dream about food. The goats and "Big Turk" disappeared. Our parents had to sell them to afford to buy oatmeal and grain. With the last of the money, our daddy bought seed potatoes from the Proprietor's store, and planted them. We watched that strip of land every day, until at last tiny green shoots began to appear. Surely, everybody thought, there would not be a blight two years running. But in the early summer, the leaves turned black, as if they had been burnt. The young stalks, just beginning to show the blossom, shrivelled and fell flat on the ground. There would be no potatoes again this year. But now, there was nothing left to sell. We had no money. It was the same over the whole country.

Our Proprietor had shut up his big house and gone to live in London with his family. A day came when there was nothing to eat. Our father went down to the shore to gather mussels, but one of the Proprietor's men was keeping guard there, with a

gun, and sent him away. The mussels belonged to the Proprietor, the man said. We all cried.

The man with the gun had told our daddy that free corn-meal was being given out in the big village down the coast. Next day my father walked ten miles there and ten miles back, in the rain, and returned with a little bag of yellow meal.

"This is Indian corn." he said.

Our mammy did not know how to prepare Indian corn, but she boiled it up in the pot, and it made a sort of gruel. We were so hungry we ate it all without noticing what it tasted like.

To get a few pennies a day, and pay for the corn,

our daddy had to work at road-building. The Proprietor, far away in London, had arranged for a road to be built up through the valley, and the government paid for half the cost. But when daddy became sick, he could not work, and he got no pay. Our mammy went down to the road-works, and she carried stones to be broken up, while daddy lay in the house and coughed and coughed.

There was no more Indian corn meal given out, but down beside the Big House a soup kitchen was set up. Inside, there was a great big pot on a fire, kept boiling all day, and at dinner time, bowls of thin, watery soup were given out. We had to go down to the soup kitchen to be given it. I led Bridget and Brian down, and daddy came behind us, very slowly, because it was hard for him to walk.

On the third day of the soup kitchen, as we went back up the hill to our house, my daddy fell down and did not move. I sent Brian running for my mammy, and she came, with two of our neighbours. They picked up daddy and carried him home. But that night, our daddy died.

THAT was the start of the bad time. We had no food, no money. The turf stack by our house was almost used up. We used to go out on the hillside and pull up plants to take back – weeds, we had thought of them as before, like nettles and charlock – and our mother boiled them in the pot on a tiny fire. Often they made us sick.

The days went by. We were cold, and weak with hunger. Our clothes became ragged but we could not mend them. Then one day we were told we and all our neighbours had to leave our houses. We had not paid the rent, and the Proprietor said we had to go.

When his men came to put us out of our little house, my brother Brian wanted to stop them. But one of the men just pushed him aside. As we walked down the hill for the last time, we saw smoke rising. They were burning the houses so that no one else could use them. Weeds were growing in the potato-patches that had once been so neatly kept.

We walked all the long way to a town. Bridget, Brian, and I had never seen so many houses

before. We stopped at a street corner and begged for food. The worst was that not far away was a bake-house, and the smell of new bread wafted towards us. We had had nothing to eat for two days. Many people in the town were as poor and desperate as we were, but we saw others come walking or driving by, with good coats and well-fed faces. We had not been long there when a man came out from a shop and told us to go away.

"Be off," he said. "We don't want you people coming in from the country bringing dirt and disease. Go back to where you came from. We have enough hungry folk here already."

But we had nowhere to go back to.

There was a soup kitchen in the town, and though Brian and Bridget could hardly walk, we struggled there and joined the crowd. At last we came to the front of the line, and a man said: "Where's your tickets?"

We had no tickets.

"There's a new system," said the man. "You have to have a food ticket, to show you come from here. We can't feed strangers."

His eye fell on us children, and he said:

"Well, just the once. I'll get into trouble, I dare say. But never mind."

We each got a bowl of thin, lukewarm gruel, a

mixture of corn-meal, oatmeal and water. But as soon as Brian ate it, he was sick.

"My children are sick," said my mother.

"Wait till the soup kitchen shuts," said the man who had helped us. "I'll take you to the Union house. There is a doctor there, sometimes."

He took us in his cart out to the edge of the town, to a big new stone building, and led us in. I heard him arguing with the man at the door. We were frightened. At last he came back and said, "They'll take you. Though the doctor has stopped coming because they can't afford to pay him."

And so we were taken into the workhouse, and exchanged our ragged old clothes for a pauper's uniform. We were all separated. Brian was put in the boy's wing, Bridget and I were in the girls' wing. Our mother was in the women's part. But for Brian and Bridget it was too late. They were too weak and ill, and the doctor did not come. They died on the same day.

I only saw our mother on Sundays, in the chapel. There I was allowed to sit with her and to spend a few minutes with her after the service. She smiled at me and held my hand, but each time she was thinner and paler. Though her eyes were bright, they held a terrible sadness. All too soon, one of the attendants rang a bell, and I had to go back to the girls' wing.

CHAPTER SIX: A BETTER PLACE

ONE morning I was called to see the Matron of the workhouse. Her expression was blank as she sat behind her desk. She beckoned me to her. "Your mother has gone to a better place, Mary," she told me.

"She would never go without me!" I cried.

"No, child, you don't understand," she said, and her voice was gentler than usual. "Your mammy has died."

Not long after that, she called for me again, and told me I was to be taken on as a servant by Mrs Palmer.

And that is my story. I was a lucky girl, but not because of being taken away by Mrs Palmer, a cruel woman who treated me like a slave. I was lucky because though I lived in the terrible time of the Great Hunger, I did not die like so many others. I lived to see a better time.

As soon as I was old enough, I ran away from Mrs Palmer. I nearly starved again. I had many adventures, but at last I got to Cork. I worked there, until I had a few pounds put by, then I bought a ticket to cross the ocean to Canada. I have a good husband here, and my own children, Brian and Bridget. Sometimes I remember our green valley of long ago, and wonder how things are in Ireland now, and how so many people could have been left to starve and die in a land where there was enough for everyone.

Note: Mary O'Donnell is an imaginary person. But the Irish potato blight and the Great Hunger were real, and the things that happened to her and her family did really happen to millions of other Irish people.

The Great Hunger happened in the years between 1848 and 1852.